Piano Man

Poems and Prayers for Lectionary Year A

Thom M. Shuman

DEDICATION

It was my Mom
who patiently traced her finger
under the words in books
as I sounded them out
and began the
still wondrous journey of
reading, writing, and playing with
words.

It was my Mom
who held my hand
as we walked to church
on Sunday mornings,
where I began the
still wondrous journey of
living, following, discovering the
Word.

Thanks for both gifts, Mom,
this book is for you!

Contents

ACKNOWLEDGMENTS

In addition to writing liturgies for each Sunday in the lectionary year, I have tried to write what I used to call the 'Back of the Bulletin' piece. Sometimes prayers, more often poetic, they were whispers which came to me in the middle of the night, or in the shower, or in those moments of procrastination from sermon preparation, nudges (if you will) by that muse we know as the Holy Spirit. More and more I imagine the Trinity as a three-piece group – God on the drums, the Spirit playing the upright bass, and Jesus at the piano – sometimes playing a little blues, a lot of jazz, a dash of r & b, and always, always improvising as they accompany our lives. I hope you hear them playing as you read these writings from several cycles of Year A.

timepiece

stretching wearily
to get the stiffness
out of your back
after a long night
at the factory,
you dump the detritus
of your pockets
onto the polished dresser:

coins picked up off the floor
as you walked around
checking that all the doors
were shut tight;
the master key
to all the offices
in the executive suite;
the pocket lint
that has accumulated
since the last time
the uniform was in the
wash.

you take the heirloom
out of your pocket,
opening it up
to look (for the umpteenth
time during the day)
at the picture
of Spirit pasted
on the inside of
the cover;

after polishing
the crystal with your
blue bandana,
you turn it over, gently
rubbing your fingers over
the inscription
'for Dad - love XP'
and putting in the key,
you wind it, as you
have done every day
since.

climbing into bed
and pulling the covers
up over you,
you whisper to yourself,
'i wonder what would
happen
if i ever forgot to wind
that old thing?'

First Sunday of Advent

when

when the world
chops down my dreams
and i am left
with only a cracked
and crumbling stump,
come . . .
to plant that seed of faith
deep within me
that will blossom
when i least expect it;

when sin's friends
strip me naked
of my hopes,
and i stand exposed
and alone,
come . . .
with that ensemble
of joy and delight
that will knock
their socks off;

when my fears
prowl around me,
smacking their lips,
ready to pounce
and devour me,
come . . .
to welcome them
(and me!)
at your Table
where we will break
the chains of bitterness
as we feast on your peace.

come . . .
come . . .
come . . .

Second Sunday of Advent

what we are to be

to those
whose hair has
risen
on the back of their
hearts,
we are to broadcast
(gracefully modified)
seeds of hope;

to everyone
whose knees
are swollen and
wobbly
from standing at
two jobs,
we are to be
braces;

to all
whose hands
are palsied by
poverty,
we are to be
gloves
woven from skeins
of food,
warmth,
shelter.

to anyone
whose feet are
blistered
from walking the burning
bricks of foolishness,
we are to be
shoes
which will easily
slip on
for the Way.

Third Sunday of Advent

mr. sandman

in those soft, hushed
  hours of the night,
    you dream

of no one noticing
as you slip in
  to be one of us,
    and a baby cries;

of all the outsiders
being welcomed
        as if they
      knew the secret
          handshake,
    and a woman
      at a well
      feeling a shiver
      run down her soul;

of pantries in soup kitchens
        never being empty,
    of shelters being open
          24/7,
    and a little boy
        handing you his lunchbox
        packed with
          a fish sandwich;

of death
  kneeling in worship,
        offering all that it owns
        back to you,
    as Beloved folds up
    his bedclothes, and walks
      into the morning.

in those soft, hushed
  hours of the night,

you . . .

Fourth Sunday of Advent

6

newborn grace

when we long for
a dreamless sleep,
you are working
the graveyard shift
to bring us life;

when we crave
a peaceful life
(no stress, no frills,
no problems, no fuss, please!)
you are down
in the trenches,
bandaging the world's wounded
with hope,
carrying them
to the kingdom's hospital,
giving us a drink
from your deep reservoir
of reconciliation;

when we think
all that is required of us
is a riskless love,
you grow so reckless
in your passion for us
that the choir director
has to compose new pieces
for the angelic chorus;

when we are convinced
we can easily dismiss you
from our daily routines,
you tap us on the shoulder,
and hand us your newborn grace,
asking us to cradle him
in our hearts.

Christmas Eve

will we

when they went
home that night,
did they hope
the anthem would
be filed away
until three years from now,
or did the tune and words
keep running through their heads
so they couldn't fall asleep?

when they went
back to work
that night,
did they grumble
about the long hours,
the harsh nights,
the low pay with no benefits,
or did they discover
they were now herders
of hope and grace,
a thankless job
no one else would take?

when they snuck
out of Bethlehem,
keeping their faces hooded
from the searching eyes
of the soldiers,
did they forget about the star,
or was its reflection
so strong in their eyes
that it seemed
it was noontime?

when she snuggled
the infant to her breast
as her husband smuggled them
through the back alleys
to the forgotten road to Egypt,
did they wonder
if they would ever
get back home
or was the promise
so ingrained in their souls
that they knew God
would hear them crying out
for release?

when we go home
this morning,
today, tonight,
from the vigil
at the stable,
will we . . .

Christmas Day

for the innocence

for little girls
who play with dolls,
  and for those
  who are treated
  like playthings;

for little boys
who bounce balls
against a wall,
  and for those
  who curl up fetally,
  longing for the comfort
  of a womb;

for those
who do not see
another's color,
but a child of God,
  and for those
  who laugh
  at another's accent;

for those who play
in safe backyards,
  and for those
  whose playground
  is potholed by bombs;

for those who pray
before climbing into warm beds,
  and for those
  whose bedroom
  is a cardboard box;

for those
whose hearts are broken
by the suffering
they see on TV,
  and for those
  whose lives are shattered
  by indifference;

for all your children,
for the innocents
in their innocence,
we would not only pray,
    but act.

First Sunday after Christmas

blessing

leaning over to rest
　　her head against
　　the tiny one kept close
to her breast,
Mary whispered,
　　　'may the Lord bless you,
　　　　Child of my heart.'

before closing the
　　　　barn door against
　　　　the chill,
　　Joseph leaned against
　　　　the edge,
　　watching the glowing faces
　　of the shepherds as
　　　　they went back toward
　　　　　　the hills,
　　　　greeting everyone they met,
　　　　'grace to you, friend!'

as we follow the
　　　　Babe out of Bethlehem,
　　watch over us, lodging
　　　　your name deep
　　　　within our hearts,
　　filling us with your
　　　　peace.

Holy Name

12

this year

i've gotten rid
of all the junk:
chips, chocolate, cola;
the fridge is now stocked
with fruits, veggies, juice -
   this is the year
   i get into shape!

no more contrived reality,
no more glazed eyes
from watching idol wannabes;
it's public radio and tv,
it's a stack of bios from the library -
   this is the year
   i form new habits!

   but you would
   take my twisted logic
   about 'who deserves'
     and reshape it
     into compassion;

   you would
   take my bitter heart
     and fill it with
     hope and joy;

   you would
   take my hurtful ways,
     and reform them
     into acts of gentleness;

   this is the year
   you take delight
   in making me
     a servant!

New Year's Day

melter of frozen hearts

God of winter and spring:
you seek to give us
every spiritual blessing,
    turning our loneliness into fellowship,
    our despair into hope,
    our death into life.

Jesus Christ,
Powerful Word of God:
    teach us your humility;
Changeless Word of God:
    fill us with your steadfast love;
Creative Word of God:
    bring us out of the exiles we have created
    and restore us to new life.

Holy Spirit,
Melter of frozen hearts:
    you invite all who are at risk
    to take a chance on God and God's promises,
    so we might discover the One
    who keeps us safe and brings us home.

Second Sunday after Christmas

star

star light:
    when invited to ride
        in comfort and style through life,
    when tempted to take
        the path of least discipleship,
shine on that other road
we are called to take -
    worn smooth by humility,
    bordered by flowers of grace,
    winding through the brokenness
        of your heart,
    taking us to the kingdom.

star bright:
illumine the shadowed corners
of our world,
    where poverty rules with
        an iron fist;
    where injustice paces
        the corridors of power;
    where need is easily handed
        to the lost, the least, the last -
for it is in these places
we are called to walk.

in our grief,
    glisten;
in our sadness,
    shimmer;
gleam with hope, with joy,
    with peace, with grace:
        star light,
            star bright,
                only star for our life.

Epiphany

morning dove

one morning,
when the Spirit,
   laughing in delight at
      the stunned look on the face of
            chaos,
         drifted across the
            waters,
   mountains thrust upward
      trying to kiss
         the man in the moon,
rivers raced one another
      to the sea, leapfrogging
            over the valleys,
   a lion's roar
      first shattered the night
            and a lamb's frightened
         bleat awoke its
               mother;

on another morning,
         a dove glides gracefully
over the Jordan, dipping down
         to kiss Jesus
      on the lips,   while
         a tremor runs through
            the hearts of the unjust,
      a death row inmate hollers
            to the guards
         to find her suitcase,
      a mother looks out
         the kitchen window, wondering
      where her son has gone
               now;

on our morning,
            at the edge of the Jordan,
      whether daintily toe-testing
            the temperature,
         dashing away, frightened by
               the slow current,
         jumping in feet first with a
            exultant yell,

walls in Gaza and Belfast
can come tumblin'
down,
polluted wells can slake
the thirst of the parched,
first graders can take the hands
of the bullies,
and sing 'ring around the rosie,'

while a puffin
coos 'alleluia.'

Baptism of the Lord/Ordinary Time 1

look!

the weakling
    who can
    topple
those immense barriers
      of distrust and
    fear
we have thrown up;

the softie
    who can gather
      up our tangled
    lives
to weave a gentle
    comforter,
    to wrap us in
      hope's warmth
against pain's bitter
    winter;

the innocent
    who sings quiet
    lullabies,
      counterpoints
to the raging cries
    of loss
    and doubt;

look!

    the
      Lamb,
who takes us
    just as we are.

Second Sunday after the Epiphany/Ordinary Time 2

slowpoke

a dawdler by
    nature,
a straggler by
    avocation,
    i could manage
        to lose a race
to a pro
    crastinator;

me-lingering through
        life,
i barely can
    find the energy
to get up and do
    nothing
    constructively;

strolling down the
        street,
    stopping at the
outdoor cafe at
    the corner of
    apathy and inert,
i while away
    my hours, making
    a cup of expresslow
        last all afternoon;

but immediately?

immediately!

that's the
    scariest
word
        in the
    Book.

Third Sunday after the Epiphany/Ordinary Time 3

19

baditudes

i could come carrying the
            ashes
of my arrogance,
handing them to
            you,
waiting expectantly
(just ignore the tap, tap, tap
of my foot)
            for you to
            recycle them into a plaque
with my name etched in
            bronze;

i could come
            with crocodile tears
            (running down my cheeks)
about how the world
            operates,
            even as i continue
            to gain from the
predicaments of
            others;

i could come sitting down
            at the table reserved
in the quiet corner,
ordering the special of the day:
filet of bias (medium well),
mashed meanness,
a medley of injustices sauteed
            in herb butter,
            followed by apple pie
            ala marred.

or
i could simply follow the
    Blesseds,
 carefully placing
 my feet in the
   tracks
  they leave behind
   in the muck and mud,
 as they wander through that
    kingdom
   they can see
  with their eyes shut
 tight.

Fourth Sunday after the Epiphany/Ordinary Time 4

halite

while there may be
(roughly)
14,000 uses for
salt,
our preference
is to use it
the same way
we have always done . . .
as a
preservative,
successfully inhibiting any
chances of
growth;

but you,
knowing that
we carry within us
particles from
creation's seas,
would have us
enhance
the world
around us.

we've removed all those
bright, old-fashioned,
incarnation bulbs,
replacing them with
CFLs
(ContemporaryFaithLite)
anticipating we will
see savings (in the first
year alone)
of some
22%;

but you,
   watching the shadows
      creep across the kingdom's
         lawn,
   would have us
   turn up the dimmer (all
         the way)
      on the walls of our
         souls,
   so others might
   be able to
      see what your
   fuss
is all about.

(halite is the mineral form salt comes in)

Fifth Sunday after the Epiphany/Ordinary Time 5

the media trumpets
  loud and clear
that i can get a hall pass
    during my marriage
  or i can have a friend
    with benefits along the way,
but you whisper the words
    commitment
      honor
        covenant
in those moments of
  weakness;

this morning
  i was told that the
     terror threat
    is as high as it's ever
    been,
so my suspicion level
  needs to be turned up
    with that sharp eye
out for packages,
    parked cars
  certain people (who
     might just look
    like you),
but your songs have lyrics full of
  reconciliation
    trust
     acceptance;

that little imp
sits on my shoulder and
  whenever i find myself
  in an awkward spot,
 not sure about what i should
   say,

he weaves a story
which wins the trophy
at the liars club convention,
urging my tongue to give it a
try,
but you keep holding up
the flash card reading
'yes'
pushing me time and again
to get it right.

Sixth Sunday after the Epiphany/Ordinary Time 6

satyagrahi*

you invite us
　to walk the streets
　　　of the world,
　　using those muddy paths
　　　marked 'kingdom'

so that when one acts
　　　with violence
　　　towards us, we will
　take gentleness out of
　　　　our clenched pockets,
　　to balm the hand injured
　　　by our face;

so when one hauls us
　into small claims court
　　　trying to get half
　of what we own,
　we will strip our homes
　of everything, loading it into
　　　their empty souls;

so when we see a homeless
　　family sitting by the
　　　side of despair,
　our generosity will turn
　　anti-panhandling laws
　　　　into toothless
　　folly.

what a dangerous invitation
　　　you send to us!

　how will we rsvp?

(c) 2011 Thom M. Shuman

* a satyagrahi is a practitioner of satyagraha,
the soul-force or firm love advocated by Gandhi.
The purpose of a satyagrahi is not to shame or
coerce the practitioner of oppression, violence,
or other manipulative acts, but to convert them
by one's practice of active non-violence.

Seventh Sunday after the Epiphany/Ordinary Time 7

alterations, no charge

last night,
i hung up my worries
in the closet,
    hoping the wrinkles
    would smooth out
    by the next day;
i put my fears
into the laundry,
    so they would
    be clean enough
    to wear again this week;
i made sure that
pebble called stress
was still in my shoe,
    where it has worn
    a hole into the heel.

but this morning,
when i opened the closet,
    i found
    a whole new outfit,
        woven out of
        Easter lilies
        and resurrection's
        sweet grass
    and sandals
    made out of
    sparrow's feathers.

  turning,

i found you
standing there,
        a tape measure
        around your neck,
        chalk in your hand,

saying with a smile,
'try them on . . .
    so we can see
    if any alterations
    are needed'

Eighth Sunday after the Epiphany/Ordinary Time 8

signs

spooning with my
            children
as they fall asleep,
      let them hear
      the deep breathing
            of your peace;

sitting around
            the kitchen table
passing platters and bowls
      to each other,
may we tell the stories
            of your grace
      which echoed in our lives;

as we travel on
            vacation,
playing 'i spy,'
      we would name
      the wonders of
            your creation;

when we step
            out of the shower
and wipe the
steam off the
            mirror,
we glimpse your
            hope
      etched on our foreheads.

Ninth Sunday after the Epiphany/Ordinary Time 9

a handfull

it it was only
in the mist-ery of
            unknowing,
   we would never have
      enough
knowledge to understand
            what in the world
   is going on with you;

if it was only
 the thundering voice
   echoing off mountain
  walls,
 we could never have enough
   silence to hear you;
if it was only
 in the sun and stars
  heaving and
   twisting
  in birth's throes,
 we could never have enough
   light to see you.

but in you
  coming
 to touch us with
  a gentle hand
  on the shoulder,
 lifting us to our feet, whispering
  'don't be scared! look...'
as you point to
  God
 standing in the kitchen,
 flour freckling the calloused hands
  kneading the dough &
  shaping it into life
   all too easily broken,
 while watching the Spirit
merrily stomping down the
      grapes of wonder,
  laughing in delight
   as grace stains the hem
 of glory's garment.

a crumb
 a sip,
  a handful of
 God

and that's more than
 enough.

Transfiguration of the Lord

29

smudged

some folks
prefer the dry rub
        method,
    the dusty ashes
    slowly drifting down
        to freckle the nose,
            gray the beard
                (a little more!)
            cause the tiniest,
            and politest,
    of sneezes from the
        little girl holding tight
            to dad's hand,
    saucer eyes on the
        thumb of the pastor;

me,
            i like a little sauce
    with mine (usually some
            evoo binding the gritty
            parts that refused to dissolve
    into the hoped-for condition),
    making it easier to smear
        on the foreheads of the
            knotted teenagers
    (can you imagine the texts
            after the service?)
    or on the back of hands
        of those who are not
        that sure of 'showing off
            their faith';

a little smudged
    suits most folks,
            and even if it takes
        a little extra elbow grease
    to rub off the evidence,
            that's usually okay . . .
    . . . but i probably
        better forget the idea
    of adding just a drop
            or three
        of permanent ink
    next time around!

Ash Wednesday

blame game

it's the snake's
fault
        you see . . .

that's why
i look at the outcasts
    with a chill-carved face,
that's why i offer the poor
soup full of rocks;

it's that snake,
you see . . .

coiling around me,
whispering that i
    am on my own,
no One
to guide me,
no One
    to follow;

it's him, you see . . .

crafting money, power,
success into icons
that slip so comfortably
into my pocket, my dreams,
        my life;

yet,
in the wilderness
the tester wears my face,
    offering me
        petty pride,
    dubious hopes,
        faithless fears . . .

if only i
    could
blame the snake!

First Sunday of Lent

31

piano man

at the bar, where
he's been nursing his wounds
   after a long bored meeting,
Nick pushes himself to his feet,
wandering over to
   the cigarette-scarred
     piano
       where Jesus is
     slowly plinking
       out
   'in the still of the night'

putting a dollar
in the chipped glass,
he begins to chat
   with the guy
   who can do wonders
     with just a few notes;

nodding slowly,
listening carefully,
   Jesus looks up
      and smiles:
'my man,
you need a new dance partner!'
   nodding to the corner;

as Nick turns,
he sees Spirit
waiting with open arms

'but, Nick,'
     Jesus whispers,
'you gotta let her lead . . .'

as he swings into
a bluesy
  'i could have danced
    all night'

Second Sunday of Lent

bucket list

each morning,
i fill my bucket
at the Well of Sin,
   and by the time
   i get halfway through the day,
     i have to turn around
     to get more;
will you meet me there
to fill me with salvation?

in the middle of the night,
i find my bucket
overflowing
from nightmares;
   will you meet me
   at the Well of Dreams
     to tell me every hope
     you have for me?

in the silence of my soul,
i discover that bucket
called my heart
   is cracked by the heat
     of my anger,
   is holed by the hurts
     of others;

will you meet me
at the Well of Grace,
   to refresh me
   with healing's
     flowing stream,
   to fill me
   with the nectar
     of sweet life?

Third Sunday of Lent

anointed one

when i would kneel
to be anointed
from the horn of hubris,
    you throw mud
    in my eyes,
        so i can see
        those trampled
        by a world stampeding
        toward success;

when i would
splash on
pomposity's perfume,
    you sprinkle me
    with the tears of children
    who,
        cradled in hunger's arms,
        cry themselves to
            sleep;

when i would
soak my feet
in the salts
of self-absorption,
    you massage them
    with the dust
    from the souls
        of the mothers walking
        along weary's highway
    to their third jobs.

anoint me,
Lord God,
that i might serve
my sisters and brothers.

Fourth Sunday of Lent

lazarus

handcuffed
  by those foolish
         fears
    we have of being
    left on our own,

swaddled
  in the cool embrace
       of our misunderstandings
    about why he came,

hampered
  by the chains
       of sin and death
     dogging him every
          step,

he stands weeping at
the now-empty tomb
            until
    he hears the Voice
         cry out,
  'unbind him and let him go . . .

         . . .to Jerusalem'

and he turns
  and goes,
         hoping not to
      stumble
  along the way.

Fifth Sunday of Lent

you

glory
is left behind,
hanging in the closet
gathering Adam & Eve's dust,
   as you put on
   humility's shirt
     (stained with grace)
   that's been lying
   crumpled up on the floor
      to be tossed into
      baptism's wash;

you
(who waded
splashing and laughing
in Eden's crystal fountain)
   now
   jump feet first
   into this messy muck
     we call life;

you
could be dancing
with the stars,
gliding around
Saturn's rings,
   but you throw
   your leg
   over the back
   of an animal
     (which reminds you
     of your disciples);

you

we welcome
with cheering voices
   and nail-choked hearts.

Palm/Passion Sunday

come Monday

Jesus groaned
getting out of bed,
trying to stretch out
the stiffness and tenderness
from riding that donkey;

hungry enough
to eat a donkey,
he grumbled under his
breath
when the service
was so lousy at
his usual eatin' place;

wanting to find
some silence and solace
he wandered into
church,
and wailed with grief
when he saw
that it had become
so upmarket
that those
who needed it
most
were not to be found;

come Monday . . .

Holy Monday

37

come Tuesday

the Morally Superior
store
was back in business,
selling conspiracies
(buy 1, get 1 free),
fear (one size fills all),
and a variety of nails,
3/shekel;

people stood around
with their hearts
in their pockets,
listening to stories
again
and,
as usual,
missing the punch line;

stubborn-souled Jesus
gently,
softly,
hopefully,
reminded folks
(once again)
that it is all about
relationships,
not rules, regs, rituals.

come Tuesday . . .

Holy Tuesday

come Wednesday

the world stunk
with the bitterness
of intrigue;
the foul breath
of secret machinations
fogged the alleys
and byways
of the city,
while the silent
walls echoed
with
the whispers
of the lovers
of shadows.

the spines of the scolds
stiffened
and dander filled
their mouths
as they took umbrage
with the one
who spread solace
on the soul
of her Beloved,
when they
would have doused him
with the sour perfume
of self-righteousness.

come Wednesday . . .

.

Holy Wednesday

come Thursday

the powers-that-be
were being themselves,
lining up lackeys
to do their dirty work;
taking money
from petty cash
to pay a bribe
under the table;

Jesus was up early
working out his frustrations
as he kneaded the bread,
letting the grace
rise to a double measure;

decanting the wine,
he giggled
as the rich bouquet
of hope (with just a hint
of promise)
filled the room;

shaking the wrinkles
out of the tablecloth
(cross-stitched
with the names of all
who had eaten with him
over the years),
he spread it over
the scarred table.

now,
everything was ready

come Thursday . . .

Holy Thursday

come Friday

palms were stuffed
into trash cans
for the post-Passover
pick-up;

nails
were strewn
in the path
of the
cross-bearer;

little kids
stopped their games
of street ball,
pressing their backs
against shadowed
walls
as death
came striding by,
arm-in-arm
with
Pilate and Herod;

and
the silence
from his friends
was deafening;

come Friday . . .

Holy Friday

come Saturday

Mary, MM, and Sally
were rearranging
the furniture
and cleaning up
the mess
from Friday's wake;

the guys,
who found their loss
uneased
no matter how much
they consumed last night,
took double doses
of painkillers
and stumbled back
to bed;

Jesus
lay in the chill
of the darkness,
his head cradled
in God's lap,
while she stroked
his hair,
humming the
Resurrection Lullaby;

come Saturday . . .

Holy Saturday

what have you done?

what have you done
with my fears?
  i left them
  on the dresser last night
    and now,
      they are gone!

what have you done
with my death?
  it has suddenly
  disappeared,
      and i've ransacked
      the house trying
      to find it!

what have you done
with my name?
  it was ground
  underfoot
      by the taunters
      and tormentors
      of Friday . . .

my fears have become
wildflowers
in Eden's garden,
  my death
  is the tattered shirt
  now used
  to mop up spills
      at the Lamb's Table,

and my name
is that sweet whisper
in my heart,
  as you take my hand
  to dance the
  Resurrection Waltz.

Easter

upper room

from the corners
of our doubts
come the claustrophobic
mutterings:
  'it's their fault . . .
  . . . how many times . . .?'

in the solace
of the shadows,
fingers stiffen in accusation:
  'i wasn't the one . . .
  . . .you said you would never . . .!'

fear
churns the room,
as we wait for
hate's hobgoblins
to jump out, yelling,
     "BOO!!!"

then
you come,
parting our tears
  to bring us out
  of grief's slavery;

putting your finger
in our fissured faith
  to make it whole;

breathing
    "Peace"
sweet, simple
  unimaginably
    unlimited
peace . . .

Second Sunday of Easter

gps

lost,
i take
a shortcut just
  down this alley,
where anger
  and agony come
tagging after me;

wandering,
i explore the wide avenues
of the world,
  whose hope
  has been potholed
    with despair;

wondering,
  i glance at the map,
and stumble down
the next street,
  only to find sin
  standing in every
    doorway,
enticing me with its
fingers sticky
    with temptation;

then we turn down
Emmaus Road,
  where the aroma
  of fresh-baked grace
wafts out each window,
and, tapping me on the shoulder,
    you shout, 'go!'
  and race me

        home.

Third Sunday of Easter

canticle 23

my steward,
  you share with me
  all i need;
my babysitter,
  you tuck me under
  the green quilt
    of love;
my teacher,
  you lift me up
  to drink from
    serenity's fountain;
my guide,
  you point out
  the walking paths
    to hope.

when the power fails,
you take my hand,
  so i won't trip
  over the furniture
    the evil one
    has moved around
      in the darkness.
your heart,
your joy,
  are a warm shawl
    for my cold
      soul.

you whip up
a gourmet meal
  (but ask me
  to share the
    leftovers
  with those who
  never gave me
    a crumb)

you pour grace
into my heart
until it overflows,
    running down the
    kingdom's streets,
        so kids can
        splash in its
            puddles.

leniency and goodwill
tiptoe after me
wherever i go,
    until i make it
        safely
    home,
where we will live
rent-free,
    watching the sunset
    that never ends.

Fourth Sunday of Easter

the stonemason

we hand you the design
   the committee has come up
with, so that the wall will
     be laid out in that dogmatic,
     unwavering line (no doubts or
      deviations) we expect,
   but after a quick glance,
  you simply place it in the back
    of the truck and start
to work;

where we would toss
   aside
those who have
  been skipped haphazardly
    over the world's waves,
  they become the tiestones
to hold the sections together,
while those wearied from
   their struggles shape the
soft gentle curves;

untying the bandana from around
   your head,
 you quietly rub the dirt
  out of the nicks and crevices
  caused when they have been ignored,
    as you gather up the children
    and youth,
   pouring them into hollow spaces,
as the aggregate to hold
   us all together;

when we expect to
  be the pride of your
    handiwork,
 you quietly pick up the
   broken, the chipped, the left-over
 slivers we kick out of our way,
   placing them as the capstones
on the dry stone wall
you are building in the
   kingdom.

Fifth Sunday of Easter

48

spoilsport

personally
  (and please don't
  take this personally)
there are those times
when i wish i were an
      orphan . . .

then,
i could ditch
my Easter outfit
    and put on my
    all-too-human skin
        again;

then,
i could
be cranky
    without guilt
    belaboring the point;

then,
i might just enjoy
treating people
    the way they seem
    to enjoy treating me.

but nooooo!
you have to go
and make Spirit
my sibling . . .

and spoil all my sin.

Sixth Sunday of Easter

49

up in the sky!

" . . . why do you stand looking
        up toward heaven?"

we look for you,
straining our eyes
into the far country,
        our vision disrupted
        by the least, the lost,
        the little, the last
        among us;

trying to catch up,
we race after you,
turning the corner
        only to find
        a homeless family
        in our path;

we wander the streets
calling your name,
yearning to find you:
but it is only
        a single mother who turns
                and wearily smiles,
        a little girl who pirouettes
                and takes our hand;
        a street person
                who whispers 'hello' -

gone,
        but you are still here, Lord,
                help us to see.

Ascension

time

we're ready;

you know
we are ready for the power
   (we've prepared ourselves
      for oh so long)
    certain we won't abuse it
    like so many before us;
but the humility,
   the weakness,
     the foolishness
you left lying on the ground
    as if we should pick them up . . .

we would go anywhere
     for you - hop on a
bus, grab the next plane,
   spend years out on the
      field of dreams, harvesting
    a bumper crop of 'them,'
but that 1000 yards down
  to the neighbor who has
      trouble
   getting up on his ladder
to clean his gutters -
   that can't be all there is
    to the journey . . .

we have the structure
    all in place,
   everyone voted to approve
the committees, the task forces,
   the bureaucrats, the gofers
   (it was unanimous, for pete's sake!);
but committing more than 2 minutes to prayer,
    facebooking the folks at the nursing home,
  blistering our feet in the race for the shelter . . .

we're getting antsy waiting, you know;
does your watch need a new
   battery?

Seventh Sunday of Easter

the party

(having burnt
        a finger
     testing the iron)
God begins -
     phump, phump, phump -
smoothing out
        the wrinkles
        on the heirloom
                tablecloth woven
        by Hagar and Sarai;

(grabbing
     Gabe and Mike
        to help)
Jesus fits
the extra boards
into the kitchen table,
             then starts
        moving the place cards
             around
     so folks
     have to sit
        next to those
        they cannot
                stand;

Spirit
is putting
     the liturgical dancers
     through their paces
stage whispering
        'flames! flames!
        flicker like flames!'
(though not telling
             any one
     of the last-minute surprise
        she will pull);

in an upper room
             we wait . . .
        turning the invitation
     over and over
             in our hearts . . .

Day of Pentecost

nothing, but

i have no proof,
   but in the carpet
   of motley grasses
     Dusty rolls on
     stretching his back;
   in the multicolored
     leaves
   which hide the squirrels
     from his gaze,
i discover you,
   Imagination beyond compare.

it's not admissible evidence,
   but in the daughter
   who sits up all night
     while her father
     slowly sleeps
     into resurrection's arms;
   in the mother
   comforting her son
   who made the last out
     in the championship game,
i learn from you,
   Compassion's Carpenter.

there is nothing concrete,
   but in the mist
   sculling over the lake.
     in the ripples
     which lullaby
     the couple in the canoe,
   in the breath
   which cradles
   the gently sailing geese,
i feel you,
   Whisperer of life.

no proof,
no admissible evidence,
nothing concrete:
   only you . . .
     God in Community,
       Mystery in One.

Trinity Sunday

DIY

done!
my improvement project
is done!

walls framed
    out of my fickle fears,
plastered with
    my dashed dreams;

windows triple-paned
    with my desires,
flooring out of
    the finest hardheaded lumber,
roofed over
    with the wretchedness
    of my will:

so why doesn't it
feel like home?

you could hammer
a refuge for me
    in your heart;

your grace could
finely sand
    my roughened edges;

your tenderness
could warm
    my iced-over soul.

when it comes
to building a life
on faith's foundation,
    i am an unskilled laborer,
so please,

        please!

do it yourself
    (for my sake)

Second Sunday after Pentecost/Ordinary Time 9

double dare

The car is packed,
the paper is stopped,
the door is locked;
the trip we have planned for
after a lifetime of work
stretches out before us
on the horizon:
>   dare we throw away the map
>   and go down unknown roads?

The monthly report
was due 5 days ago,
the accounts do not balance,
the boss is standing
over my cubicle, tap-tap-tapping
his fingers on the wall:
>   dare i get up
>   and follow that stranger?

My physician says
it's all in my mind,
the experts tell me
there is nothing they can do,
my friends and family
insist that i learn to live with it:
>   dare i take heart
>   and reach out in trust?

Is that a double-dare
i hear, Entreating God?

Third Sunday after Pentecost/Ordinary Time 10

ordinary gifts

i long to lay hands
on my loved ones
    in the hospital,
and see them get up and walk,
healed and restored:
    but you call me
    to sit by their bed
    and hold their hand
    through the sleepless night.

i would give almost anything
to make a paste out of dirt and spit,
to rub it on the eyes
of my neighbor who is sightless,
and witness her joy
at seeing sunrise for the first time:
    but you call me
    to read a book
    with a child
    who stumbles over the words.

i would like to win the lottery
so i could give the money away
to improve the lives
of all those
saturated with poverty:
    but you call me
    to help frame walls
    for a Habitat family.

may i take all the ordinary gifts
you have given me,
Exuberant God,
and use them
where you send me.

Fourth Sunday after Pentecost/Ordinary Time 11

heart to heart

i must admit that,
while not bodily,
i know what it is like
to be cast out
by people i thought
cared for me:
   ridiculed by a parent,
   rejected by a lover,
   downsized by an employer,
   gossiped about by a friend.

wandering
pain's wilderness,
   feeding on my bitterness,
     alone
        forsaken
           forgotten

until you
bent over to hear
   the breaking of my spirit
     and my tears
     striking the rock garden
     planted in my soul

and you
wiped away my anguish
with the Spirit's waters,
   lifting me up,
   holding me tight
in your own
   broken heart.

Fifth Sunday after Pentecost/Ordinary Time 12

who forgives God?

when
  in that hedgerow
  woven tight with the
    vines of despair,
      the thorns of loss
      pricking at us,
  we find no ram
  caught by its horns;

when
  we cling desperately to
    each other as our
      child is wheeled
      towards the surgery,
    where her life is placed
    in the hands of strangers,
  and no angel comes
  running down the hall, yelling
      'wait!'

when
    we have mailed the letter
  to that old friend whose
      heart our anger broke
      all those years ago,
    but no word of pardon comes;
when
  the doctor comes into
    our room, but the words
    uttered are not
  "it's benign";
when
  there is no last minute
      reprieve
    in the sentence of
    loneliness
  which has been pronounced
      upon us;

when,
  do we forgive

      you?

Sixth Sunday after Pentecost/Ordinary Time 13

treading

treading in the sea
of stress

    my bones
    fall asleep
    as i put in my time
    at work;

    my eyes glaze over
    as i stare
    at the demands
    on my calendar;

    my brain rebels
    at storing
      one more event,
      one more task,
      one more meeting;

too tired
to be tired
  i yearn:

to hear
your invitation
of rest,

to be yoked
to your healing love,

to lie down
in shalom's caress.

Seventh Sunday after Pentecost/Ordinary Time 14

canticle 119:105-112

your grace is a lamp to my feet:
   lighting my way
   through the shadows
   my sin casts;

i was baptized
and affirm those promises:
   to honor your tenderness;

i struggle with
my soul's pain:
   so fill me with life,
   Tender Heart,
      for you will
      compassion;

i lift my songs of joy
to you, Hope's Home:
   opening my spirit
   to your generosity;

holding my life
in my trembling hands,
   i remember:
      you cradle me
      in your love;

the world tries to seduce
me from your kingdom,
   but i stick close
   to your kindness;

your goodness and mercy
were my gifts at birth:
   they continually fill my soul;

i lean my heart
towards yours,
   that i might live
   your grace
      through all eternity.

Eighth Sunday after Pentecost/Ordinary Time 15

canticle 139

you thought for a moment,
and creation sprang forth
from your Wisdom;

    and now,
    you know my thoughts:
        anger that can
            crush another's spirit;
        contempt that can
            drown a dream;
        hatred which could
            cripple a lover.

you spoke a Word,
and healing walked
among death's dark shadows;

    and now,
    before i can say a word,
    you know
        the loneliness
            stalking my nights;
        the sin
            corroding my heart;
        the emptiness
            flooding my soul.

you know

and yet
    you reach out
    to grasp my hand,
    walking with me
so that
    at last,
        i am finally with you.

        Ninth Sunday after Pentecost/Ordinary Time 16

in our midst

the kingdom of heaven
  is like an old dog
  curled up in a
      sunbeam
    snoring his praise
    in solitude;

the kingdom of heaven
  is like a seashell
  burrowed under the beach
    which a little girl
      found
    and gave to her best
      friend
    in the bleak midwinter;

the kingdom of heaven
  is like a
      sprinkle of
    fireflies
  skimming across the
     lawn, just
   out of the
       reach
  of dancing
    kittens;

the kingdom
    is . . .

Tenth Sunday after Pentecost/Ordinary Time 17

ebb and flow

laughing and chatting,
piped aboard by
flutes of champagne,
the crowd pours onto
the chartered liner
for the crossing,
   tables groaning with
   the finest food;
   nine-piece band
   tuning up for the dancing;
   the captain waiting,
   tanned, smiling, nodding,
   promising a gentle crossing;

down the beach,
i clamber
into the rickety rowboat,
   paint faded into a dull gray,
   water sloshing in the bottom,
   the seat stained and creaky,
   the shipshape shaky;

you hand me
the nicked and cracked oars,
and noticing the askance
on my face, whisper,
'look, this way
you get to know the water,
   its ebb and flow,
   the tides that can
      rip out your heart,
   the rocks lurking beneath
      the smooth glass,
   the way the surface can
      change in an instant;'

pushing me out into the water,
you continue,

'it's harder, i know . . .
i've done it myself.'

Eleventh Sunday after Pentecost/Ordinary Time 18

as if

as if
it were so simple
to believe:
    when i am offered
    a smorgasbord of choices
    by the culture around me;

as if
it were as elementary
as confessing:
    when i am taught
    that everything i do
    is exactly the right choice
       for me!

as if
it were easy
to get out of the boat,
    when i rest so
    comfortably in the bottom,
    rocked to sleep
       by apathy's lullabies;

as if
it were a piece of cake
to walk on faith's
crashing waves:
    when everyone is
    grasping and clutching
    to keep me from taking
    such a foolish step . . .

if only
i could live
 'as if . . .'

Twelfth Sunday after Pentecost/Ordinary Time 19

no more waiting

she had heard
of those promises made
under starry, sable skies:
    blessings flowing
    through the lines
    of desert wanderers,
        which would bring life
        to every one
        of God's children;

she had heard
of this wandering band
of foolish followers
    led by the teacher
    who reminded his kin
    of those long-ago
    spoken covenants;

but she was tired of
hearing only words . . .

even if it was only
crumbs,
    she wanted to be fed
    from grace's table;
even if it was only
a glance,
    she wanted Jesus
    to see her as
    his sister;
even if it was only
a whisper,
    she longed for him
    to call her daughter
    'my niece'.

the waiting was over . . .

Easter's Child had come
to her heart.

Thirteenth Sunday after Pentecost/Ordinary Time 20

Q & A

when it shows up
on the test
('who do you say I am?')
i quickly flip open the book
and copy out the answers . . .

for
'Son of the living God'
has become a research paper
(hopefully expanding into
a dissertation)
with experts, writing
in several languages,
quoted to support my view,
    but a real Person:
        calling me to follow;
        willing to open my shut mind;
        hoping to send me out
            to confront the powers
            in my corner of the world?

and
i have said
'Lord'
so many times
that i have lost count,
    but the instances
    i have (actually,
    willingly, eagerly)
    given you control of my life?
        even if i include the
        thumb on my counting hand,
        i still have several fingers
        left over . . .

so maybe i need
to close the book,
and open my self
  to you.

Fourteenth Sunday after Pentecost/Ordinary Time 21

easier

it's a whole lot
    easier
      to lose my cross,
    than to lose my life;
to leave it propped
    up against the corner
  of the closet, dust
      bunnies sleeping
    at its feet;
to ignore it
    standing on the coffee
  table, looking out the front
      window, its cow eyes
    brimming with tears,
  as i pull away from
  the curb;
to simply reply, 'i can't
  remember the last time
    i saw it,' when
    i'm asked, 'what ever
  happened to your cross?'
but
each morning, it puts
    Good
  into my hands,
  closing my fingers tight
    over it, whispering,
    'don't let go; don't ever
    let go.'
it tapes a picture of evil
    to my bathroom mirror,
  so i will know it
    when i see it,
  and stand up to it;
it spends each lonely day
  at the loom,
    weaving the yarns
  labeled hope, love,
    patience, perseverance
    into that community
  which helps me to
    bear what is mine.

Fifteenth Sunday after Pentecost/Ordinary Time 22

gathered

we gather in this place, warm, safe, secure,
trusting and believing you are with us;

they gather,
huddling together for
warmth, worrying about
who might prey
on them next,
in cities that don't care
about their lost children;

they gather,
trying to hold their
families together,
knowing that after
48 hours, they must
leave the shelter they
call home;

they gather,
shuffling their feet,
trying not to lose their
place in line,
peeking over the shoulders
of those in front of them,
hoping there will be enough
bread and soup;

they gather,
passing the bread and the cup
to the next person in the circle,
holding hands and praying
for the wisdom, the grace,
the peace, the privilege
of going out to serve those
who are lost more than they are found,
who would consider the least abundance,
who trail behind those in last place,
who are so little in the eyes of the world
they are never seen.

Lord, keep your promise
to be with us
wherever we gather.

Sixteenth Sunday after Pentecost/Ordinary Time 23

F word

leery
of becoming a
97-pound weakling,
i regularly exercise my
    umbrage
at those who have done
wrong to me . . .
        but you would release
        my death grip
        on pain's weights,
    and give me
    a Spirit-filled bouquet
    of mercy's tender flowers
        to hand out
        as i walk home.

watching
the line form of
all who can't wait
to wipe bitterness on my soul,
i hesitate to open my heart
to put out the welcome mat,
    but you sweep off
    the sidewalk
    to make a way for them,
        leading to the porch
        where a pitcher of
        cool refreshing leniency
        has been poured for them

have patience, Lord,
    have patience:
till i discover
forgiveness
is not a word listed
in the world's lexicon
of foolish notions,
        but grace gifted
    over
        and over
            and over
to me.

Seventeenth Sunday after Pentecost/Ordinary Time 24

payday

we know how the world operates:
   you work hard,
      you pay your dues,
         you show up early and leave late,
            you sacrifice your family, your values,
            your self on the shrine of stress.

then,

you come along,
upsetting the applecart
we have stacked so carefully
with all our expectations,
all our assumptions,
all we have been taught

handing every single one of us
the very same gift;

and you walk away,
your hands stuffed
into your empty pockets,
softly humming 'Amazing Grace'
under your breath,

as you leave us
with our jaws
scraping the ground.

Eighteenth Sunday after Pentecost/Ordinary Time 25

complaint dept

as the doors open
and the folks begin
to take numbers and line up,
he wanders around
   kneeling to put a smile
   on a cranky child's face;
      soothing a mother worried
      about catching the bus for work;
         leaning over to hear
         the frustrated grandfather
         on his fifth visit this week.

as the crowd snakes out the door,
the metal-shuttered window
flies up with a bang
and the baggy-eyed woman
who has been running
the department forever
(will she ever retire?)
   leans her leathery elbows
   on the scarred counter
   and calls out 'number 1!'
      nodding,
         smiling,
            grimacing,
               comforting
she listens to each one,
and whispers (at the end)
to each to go around the corner . . .

. . . where they find a kiosk
carved from stone
   where the perky, young
   attendant smiles
and hands out a drink
of crystal clear water,
laughing,
   'here! this is what you've
   been looking for all along!'

Nineteenth Sunday after Pentecost/Ordinary Time 26

vineyard

maybe we ought
to form a tenants' rights
    organization,
    Owner of the Vineyard;

after all,
we seem to be doing
    a pretty good
    job
    with what you have
        given to us:

so
what do we need
with all those
        servants
    you keep sending our way:
        Mother Theresa,
            Taize's Roger,
            Martin Luther King, Jr.,
    and all the others
    who don't seem to have a
        clue
        as to how to run
        a vineyard?

if you aren't careful,
we might discover that
    humility is preferred
        over power;
    service is more seductive
        than success;
    wisdom is to be more treasured
        than wealth.

and then what will
        happen
    to what you have
        created?

Twentieth Sunday after Pentecost/Ordinary Time 27

the reception

in his off-the-rack
        tux
    and too-tight shoes,
    Jesus fidgets at the
            door,
    glancing at his watch
            every few minutes
    (always surprised that an
    hour hasn't passed since
    the last time he looked),
        peering, once more,
            down the road
            for signs of the
            stretch limos;

back in the kitchen,
    steam roiling around
    like cumulus clouds,
            Spirit
        mutters to the sous-chef,
    her breath sending the
            chefs de partie
            fluttering around,
                checking sauces,
                keeping salads crisp,
                banging lids and
                turning down flames,
        doing their best to avoid
            her look;

having polished the flatware
            for the hundredth time,
    and centered the arrangements
        for the last time,
            Abba
        sighs behind the bar,
    watching the fluted champagne
    flatten minute by minute;

throwing the bar towel down,
   the long-sufferer stomps
      to the back door and
      flings it open, hollering,
  'you cardboard box dwellers,
   you dumpster divers,
   you panhandling pariahs -
         come on in!
      there's plenty for all;
      bring your buddies!'

Twenty-first Sunday after Pentecost/Ordinary Time 28

play-acting

having taken
the Hypocritic Oath,
i can easily prescribe
a treatment of behavior
for my neighbors,
yet proscribe
the same ethics
from my life;

switching sides
as easily as a
charlatan
changes his beliefs,
i can make reservations
for a pious table,
and gorge myself
at temptation's buffet;

building my image
as a purveyor of peace,
i can dissemble
with violent thoughts
and the WMDs of words;

please:
hold up that shiny coin
which bears my image
so i can see
who i really am,
and discover
whose i might be . . .

Twenty-second Sunday after the Pentecost/Ordinary Time 29

how

how do
i love you
when my mind
is so easily distracted
   by the yelling on television,
   the anger on the roadways,
   the dullness of my life?

how can
i love you
when my heart
is so broken by
   the hatred among believers,
   the bitterness of friends,
   the forgiveness which eludes me?

how should
i love you
when my soul
   thirsts for a companion,
   hungers for empathy,
   longs for a respite from its weariness?

maybe,
just maybe,
if i stop hanging on
to all my questions,
let go of all my answers,
and be caught by your grace,
i will be able to love
YOU
with all i am,
all i have,
all i hope to ever be.

Twenty-third Sunday after the Pentecost/Ordinary Time 30

practice

if we practiced
what we preach,
O God:

our pockets
would be empty,
and the poor
would be Citizens of the Year;

our waistlines
would be thinner,
and the hungry
would not have to stand
in soup lines;

our pride
would be thrown out
with the rest of our garbage,
so we could shoulder
the burdens of the broken.

give us more time to practice,
Gentle Teacher,

not so we could
become perfect,

but that our deeds
would become
permanent.

Twenty-fourth Sunday after Pentecost/Ordinary Time 31

for each and every one

for Columba, Phoebe, Hild, Cuthbert,
Ninian, Brigid and all the faithful
who kept the Light of Christ alive
in the darkest of moments;

for Thomas Merton, Dorothy Day,
Brother Roger, Mother Theresa, and
all those who remind us that our
calling is still to that sainthood
which serves, which prays,
which listens, which gives;

for Teddy, for Joel, for Justin, for Artiffany:
for all those differently-gifted saints
through whom God has blessed us
with laughter, with joy, with grace,
with a glimpse of the kingdom;

for the Millers, Fred White, Billy
Wireman, Eleanor Pugh, Wellford Hobbie,
John Trotti, Betty Achtemeier, and all
the other mentors of my life;

for all those who this day choose
to entertain angels rather than
be stimulated by our culture;

for all those who today will let go
of their wants in order to serve the
need of another;

for all those who tonight will sit
by the bed of the dying, rather than
resting in their own sleep;

for all those who tomorrow will try
to be faithful, again, in following
Jesus:

for all the saints,
we give you thanks,
Precious God,
we give you thanks.

All Saints' Day

78

as for me

it was not
so long ago
i served other gods:
   years ago, it was named 'fear';
   last month, i kneeled at greed's altar;
      this past week, pride seduced me;
   yester (& almost every) day
      i followed anger down
that potholed road.

even when
i put them away
in a box marked
   'former life,'
they try to
slip their fingers
under the edges
   to push the lid off -
or swaddle themselves
in red and green ribbon,
   so i will find them
   under the tree;

so
for this day and
   (please, Lord!)
all the days to follow,
i will choose
to cross faith's River,
   leaving them
   on the shoreline
behind me.

Twenty-fifth Sunday after Pentecost/Ordinary Time 32

talents

as the brown truck
pulled away from the
     curb,
  i picked up
  the box left
    on the porch,
and recognizing the
return address,
     i immediately
  repackaged it in
     foil and
  plastic wrap, placing
it in the bottom of the
  basement freezer,
     knowing no thief
would look for faith
     there;

when i found the
  present way at the back
  of all the ones
     under the tree,
and saw whose name
  was on the gift tag,
  i told the rest of the
     family i'd open
     it after dinner,
but while everyone was
dozing off in front of
  the tv, i carried it
     up to the attic,
and hung grace way in
  the back of Aunt Maude's
     wardrobe that's been
  in the family for decades;

standing at the counter,
my back blocking your view,
as you told me, 'cream
and two sugars,'
i added something else
to your tea, and when
you fell asleep, i picked
you up and carried
you out into the night,
hiding you in the compost
of my fears
and doubts,
hoping you would never

notice.

Twenty-sixth Sunday after Pentecost/Ordinary Time 33

meeting place

when you sit
with the homeless
at the local shelter,
you are enthroned in glory,
surrounded by the angels
we have forgotten;

when you pass
the bread
at the downtown soup kitchen,
you bless it
with your grace,
that your neighbor
might be filled with hope;

when you take off
your winter coat
and drape it around
a shivering child,
she is warmed
by your heart
aflame with compassion;

we wonder why we cannot find you,
when we search for you
among the powerful and wealthy,
while all along you have been with
the citizens of your Kingdom:
the hungry, the naked, the sick,
the imprisoned, the lost, the lonely.

help us to meet you there,
Lord Jesus,
help us to meet you there.

Reign of Christ/Christ the King

always

you give us the
                first fruits
        of your grace:
                friends who come to our
                        door
                with a hot meal when
                we return from the hospital,
                a stranger who starts our
                                car
                on a rainy morning;

you offer us the
                first fruits
        of your love:
                teenagers who shovel our
                        walks
                after the first snowfall (waving
                        off our attempts to pay),
                children singing impromptu
                        songs of joy
                at the bus stop;

you hand us the
                first fruits
        of your hope:
                neighbors who throw a
                house-warming party for
                        the immigrant family
                who just moved in,
                Bread which nourishes our
                        souls
                so we might open
                our pantries when the food
                        collection is held at work.

we remember how
                you
        always provide for us
                and we would rejoice in
                        all ways.

Thanksgiving Day

prayer for Memorial/Remembrance Day

We remember, Grieving God,
those, in so many places,
in so many times,
who have died in war;
   and we pray
   we might honor them
   by becoming your children,
   makers of peace to our broken world.

We remember, Mothering God,
children who have grown up
around us in our schools,
in our neighborhoods, in our churches,
and who have now gone to war;
   and we pray for children
   throughout the world
   who are the orphans
   of violence and death.

We remember, God of Truth,
the wars which rage within us,
the aggression we feel towards others,
our unwillingness to forgive,
our desire to foster divisions and discord,
our discomfort in being called
 to love our enemies;
   and even as we despair,
    we pray for new hope,
   as we struggle to see you in our world,
    we pray for discerning hearts,
   as we confront ancient fears,
    we pray for new love,
 and for your old, old peace
 to be born in us anew.

As we remember,
we pray, Healing God.

ABOUT THE AUTHOR

Thom M. Shuman is a graduate of Eckerd College (St. Petersburg, FL) and Union Presbyterian Seminary (Richmond, VA). Currently active in transitional/interim ministry, he has served churches in Oklahoma, Virginia, and Ohio. His liturgies, poems, and prayers are used by congregations all over the world, and by individuals for personal devotions.

His Advent devotional books *The Jesse Tree* (2005) and *Gobsmacked* (2011) have been published by Wild Goose Publications/The Iona Community (www.ionabooks.com), as well as his wedding liturgy, *Now Come Two Hearts*. *Lenten and Easter Nudges* (PDF download) was published in 2013. He is a contributor to the Iona Community's Resource books *Candles & Conifers, Hay & Stardust, Fire and Bread, Bare Feet and Buttercups,* and *Acorns and Archangels*, as well as *Going Home Another Way: Daily Readings and Resources for Christmastide, Gathered and Scattered: Readings and Meditations from the Iona Community, 50 New Prayers From The Iona Community,* and *Like Leaves to the Sun, Prayers from the Iona Community.*

Playing Hopscotch in Heaven, Lectionary Liturgies for RCL Year A is a companion to *Piano Man*.

Dusty the Church Dog and other sightings of the gospel has just been published.

Bearers of Grace and Justice, a book of liturgies with communion for Lectionary Year C was published in 2012, as well as its companion book, *Pirate Jesus, poems and prayers for Lectionary Year C.*

He blogs at www.occasionalsightings.blogspot.com
www.prayersfortoday.blogspot.com
www.lectionaryliturgies.blogspot.com

Cover photo: © Susan P. McCamey, used with permission

Made in the USA
Lexington, KY
02 September 2014